State Month' Dital Tms

es

UNLOCKING ARIZONA'S PROPHETIC DESTINY

21 Day Devotional
Declaring God's Heart for Arizona

Deb Welch

Lite the Fire Ministries
Igniting the Generations
for
Breakthrough and Transformation

GATEWAY PRESS
A Division of Aion Group Multimedia
and Gateway International Bible Institute

Unlocking Arizona's Prophetic Destiny
21 Day Devotional
Declaring God's Heart for Arizona

Copyright 2014 by Deb Welch
Coverstock image: Jenn Huls

Published by:

GATEWAY PRESS
A Division of Aion Group Multimedia
and Gateway International Bible Institute

20118 N 67th Ave
Suite 300-446
Glendale, Arizona 85308
www.aionmultimedia.com

Printed in the United States of America

ISBN:978-0-9915657-0-2

DEDICATED TO:

Every Intercessor and Prophet that has prayed, wept and prophesied over the beautiful State of Arizona.

ACKNOWLEDGMENTS

I want to give special honor to Hal and Cheryl Sacks who have faithfully mobilized prayer in Arizona for over thirty years. Without their perseverance I don't believe Arizona would be the State it is today. On a personal note I am very thankful to the Sacks who believed in the call of God on my life and the passion in my heart to see Arizona ignited in non-stop prayer and helped make that dream become a reality.

A special acknowledgment also goes to Cindy Jacobs. I am believing for a great harvest for not only the words and time she has sown into Arizona, but also to her father who gave his life to see the Gospel preached in this state.

I want to honor every prophetic voice that has sown words of hope and destiny into Arizona, without each one of you this book would not be possible. As a State we want to be good stewards of the words of the Lord you have released. I also want to honor the prophetic voices and intercessors that have labored in the State and not given up and not left their post. My friends, I believe it is time to reap the reward!

To my husband Jack, I am so thankful for the gift of God you are to me. You challenge me and cheer me on. I am a better person because of you. I love you more!

Finally, Jesus! As the Moravian missionaries cried, "For the Lamb is worthy of the reward of His suffering." May this bring honor to Your Name!

TABLE OF CONTENTS:

INTRODUCTION

I have had the privilege of serving the Lord and Arizona, by mobilizing non-stop prayer throughout the State since New Year's Eve 2007 through a prayer initiative called "The Torch". As part of this journey, I have collected and mobilized prayer for the prophetic words that have been released over Arizona. What an amazing destiny the Lord has for the A to Z State! I have found references to Phoenix and Arizona in words from as early as 1965. This compilation is by no means meant to represent an all-inclusive list but has been published as a guide to be used to bring encouragement. My prayer is that it will be used as a resource to pray and decree Arizona's great destiny until we see these things come to pass.

In 1 Timothy 1:18, Paul admonishes Timothy to wage war with the prophetic words. *"This charge I commit to you, son Timothy, according to the prophecies previously made concerning you, that by them you may wage the good warfare."* So, what exactly does that mean? It is about getting in agreement with what heaven is saying and as intercessors we are to stand in the gap until those things that have been prophesied come to earth.

I am passionate about seeing those things spoken over Arizona come to pass. I am believing as you use this guide to pray for Arizona, you will be ignited with that same passion. I have been bold and have told the Lord I didn't want to hear about another move of your spirit somewhere else; I want to experience the fullness of what You have promised here in Arizona! I understand that some prophesies require action on our (the Church's) part, but I believe that as we continue to seed the atmosphere with these words and remind the Lord of His promises, we will see things shift and actions that need to happen will come into reality and we will see Arizona walk in her redemptive purposes.

I believe that even as we continue to pray through the prophetic words in this book we will continue to seed the heavens with God's promises. Isaiah 51:16a says, *"And I have put My words in your mouth; I have covered you with the shadow of My hand, That I may plant the heavens."*

Let us continue to decree a thing that it may be established! Job 22:28, *"You shall also decide and decree a thing, and it shall be established for you; and the light [of God's favor] shall shine upon your ways." [Amplified]*

I believe the Lord is ready to perform His word!

Day 1

Destiny Robbers – The Imprint of a False Identity

I am excited for you to start this journey of Unlocking Arizona's Prophetic Destiny as I believe it will not only bring a focused prayer storm for this state, but it will also help unlock your own personal prophetic destiny too.

This first day will be a little different from the remainder, but I felt it was important to lay a foundation for the intent. Each day a different prophetic promise will be shared, along with a short testimony or story then ending with some prayers, scripture and action steps.

Although the writing of this book has come quickly, the process unknowingly has been unfolding over the last eight years. It has been a gathering of testimonies and personal experience with the Lord as I have travelled the state mobilizing prayer. It has been an amazing journey and I am so thankful for the privilege of being able to share it with you. My prayer is that it will bless you, encourage you, challenge your faith and spur you on to love and good works. The outflow will be that Arizona is changed as the people who live here are changed because of their maturing walk with the Lord.

As I have gathered the prophetic promises, it has struck me how the enemy has tried to steal these promises and imprint a false identity upon Arizona. What others often say about our beautiful state is not what God says about it. We need to line up with the report of the Lord!

Although I have many stories I could share this one story in particular has struck me. It is the tragedy of the Granite Mountain Hotshots.

When this tragedy hit Arizona, I sought the Lord because it happened on my watch. The Lord had me research what marked these firefighters as "Hotshots". According to the definition given on Wikipedia.com, *"Hotshot crews are considered an elite group among wild land firefighters, due to their extensive training, high physical fitness standards, and ability to undertake difficult, dangerous, and stressful assignments. They often respond to large, high-priority fires and are trained and equipped to work in remote areas for extended periods of time with little logistical support."* In other words, they are forerunners.

The enemy would like us to step away from our call to be a forerunner State; to pull back, fear the fire and play it safe. But, the Lord wants us to embrace His fire; the fire of His burning love for us and to lead the way for the nation.

I remember Chuck Pierce saying that he had a vision in May, 2008 where the Lord showed him the United States. Arizona was the only state that was fully engulfed and ablaze with the glory. As you can see, the enemy would like us to pull back and fear the fire. God has a great call upon this state to lead the nation!

It's Your Turn:

Read and meditate on John 10:10.

Ask the Lord to show you where the enemy has attempted to steal your destiny and imprint a false identity.

Spend some time journaling some of the scriptures that the Lord has spoken to you and the prophetic promises you may have received. Then make a commitment to start praying those promises on a daily basis.

Day 2

Arizona Take the Point
Cindy Jacobs - June 2004

"He showed me that Arizona must take the point in the prayer for the elections. God spoke that to me. Take the point. I've been all kinds of different places, and I have not ever said that to one state yet. But I want to say to you Arizona, you have the anointing to stand this time. You can do it. I began to write and I began to take notes. This is what the Lord said to me. He said you will contend for the nation. He said the enemy hit the USS Arizona; that was a prophetic sign as to how afraid he is of Arizona. Those young men and women who went to the bottom there at Pearl Harbor are martyrs for this nation. It gives you a great right and a great authority as Arizonans to say, the enemy is not going to take any of our young men and women down anymore. The Lord has shown me, that Arizona you are warriors; that is your DNA. Wake up and become who you are. God is saying to Arizona; I'm trusting you for the nation."

I remember so vividly when this prophetic word was released. At the writing of this book, I feel like this word has become a part of my very being. This word propelled me on

5

a journey to study Pearl Harbor, the USS Arizona and the impact that December 7th, 1941 had on this nation. I have always been a student of history, especially the World War II era. I believe it is part of my calling to mobilize the prayer army to study the history and strategies of natural wars. Little did I realize the impact this research would have on my life, including taking me half way around the world to pray in both Japan and Hawaii using prophesy to heal history.

As Arizonans, we have great authority. We are warriors at heart. However, to move into a greater level of authority we have to deal with the altars we erect in times of trauma. Arizona's identity has been marked by a moment in history that has become known as a date which will live in infamy and the sinking of a ship that is named for her. The enemy will attempt to shipwreck our faith and our destiny just as he sunk the USS Arizona. BUT GOD! My belief is that our God, who released resurrection power to raise Jesus from the dead and part the Red Sea for the Hebrews, is also powerful enough to make that ship float. He is well able to release buoyant faith and resurrect dreams, callings and destinies.

It's Your Turn:

Declare aloud whenever possible:

LORD, release your resurrection power over Arizona; that she will walk in the fullness of her destiny as a warrior state in the Lord's army.

Arizona, AWAKEN to your destiny.

Arizona, take the point for this Nation.

Ask the Lord to show you if you have any traumatic experiences in your life that may have caused your faith to shipwreck. Then ask Him to release His resurrection power and faith into those places.

Day 3

Establishing the Moravian Lampstand
Cindy Jacobs – June 2000

*As I was praying, I felt that the Lord gave me a word that He wants to put the Moravian fire in this state, and that the hallmark of this state will be **24 hour prayer** and that it will be said of Arizona that there is not a moment any time of the day that someone is not lifting up the name of the Lord, crying out for renewal, crying out for mercy, crying out for visitation..."*

You may be asking, "Who are the Moravians, what is their lampstand and what does that mean for Arizona?" The Moravians were a group of Christian refugees that settled on the estate of Count Nicholas Zinzendorf in Saxony, Germany. In the beginning, the community was in disunity, fighting over doctrine. The Count appealed many times for the different groups to come together. Finally, after a great move of God in 1727 they came together and made a covenant to pray non-stop. Their motto was *"no one worked unless someone prayed"*. This prayer meeting lasted over 100 years and impacted the globe! During their prayer times they found themselves praying for obscure places like Turkey, Greenland, North Africa and the West Indies.

This community, Hernnhut, translated "Watch of the Lord" started to touch others. Two men they influenced would change the course of history in England, America and beyond. These men were Charles and John Wesley. The story is told that John was on a voyage to America as a missionary. During the voyage, he met some Moravian missionaries. On the journey, a storm arose and Wesley became afraid, but he saw the Moravians stay calm and praised the Lord and sang hymns.

They survived the journey and arrived safely in America. Later, Wesley sought out the Moravians to learn more about their relationship with the Lord that allowed them to stay in such peace during the storm. Wesley would visit their community to learn more.

At the time of the Wesley brothers, England was corrupt and godless. France was in the middle of a bloody revolution. England could have gone the same way, but instead of a revolution, England experienced the Great Awakening. An awaking that would spread to America. This was not just a revival but a move of God that changed society. Oh, how we need that in America today!

It's Your Turn:

Declare:

Lord, establish the Moravian Lampstand in this state that will ignite an awakening that will change society.

Lord, ignite a passion in us to cry out for renewal, to cry out for mercy and to cry out for a visitation. May that cry arise day and night until we see a move of Your Spirit!

Consider visiting one of the many prayer rooms around the State and spend some dedicated time with the Lord.

Day 4

The Release of a Missionary Movement
Cindy Jacobs – June 2000

"The Lord showed me that through this incredible prayer movement that is going to go on in the state of Arizona and in the valley of the Son, there will be an anointing to pray. The Lord showed me that from that place there is going to be birthed one of the greatest mission-sending movements that the world has ever seen. The Lord showed me that there's going to be hundreds and hundreds of missionaries sent from this city and from this state."

This is a continuation from Day 3. As the Moravian community prayed, they began to plan how they could go to distant places. It seemed impossible. It's not like today where you simply get on a plane to travel to another country. Their journey would take weeks or even months by ship or over land.

Five years after the non-stop prayer started, the first two Moravians were sent to the African slaves of St. Thomas, in the West Indies. The story is told that as they waved to their loved ones, knowing that they would not see them again they shouted from the bow of the ship, "The Lamb is worthy to receive the reward of His suffering".

After three years of working alongside the slaves, they had four converts. During the first four years of Moravian missions, 22 had laid down their lives in what they called the "great death." By the time Count Zinzendorf died in 1760, it is reported that the little community of Herrnhut had sent out 226 missionaries! Within one generation, they reached almost all the continents and established the modern day missionary movement.

As the 100 year prayer watch continued, they prayed for the Gospel to be carried to every country on earth.

It's Your Turn:

Lord, rise up the laborers to be sent into the harvest. Set them on fire, to walk in holiness and purity with demonstration of Your love, power and might.

"Therefore pray the Lord of the harvest to send out laborers into His harvest." Matthew 9:38

"Ask of Me, and I will give You The nations for Your inheritance, And the ends of the earth for Your possession." Psalm 2:8

If you've never been on a short term mission trip, ask the Lord to open up an opportunity for you to go somewhere that is out of your normal routine of life.

Day 5

Apostolic Training Centers
Rick Joyner & James Goll- 1989

"I had a vision of 12 cities in the US that were destined to become centers where the church at large would flock to be fully equipped for the work of the Lord. Phoenix was one of the 12." Rick Joyner - 1989

James Goll had a very similar vision where he saw a map of the US and apostolic centers. Again, Phoenix was one of them. These centers had an influence over a 500 mile radius.

In 2008, Lite the Fire launched a prayer initiative. It was the vision of a young man named Keith Barnes. His vision was to see the State of Arizona in non-stop prayer for all of 2008. Keith and I linked arms and generations and launched what we now call "The Torch". You will hear me refer to this prayer initiative several times throughout this book. (If you are interested in more information about "The Torch" Non-Stop Prayer Initiative, you can refer to the Appendix at the end of the book.)

I remember when we had finished the first year's circuit of Arizona with The Torch that the Lord started speaking to me about Apostolic Training Centers. At the time, that vernacular was not being widely used in the Body of Christ as it is at the time of this writing. I started asking the Lord what He meant and what marked such a location.

I started researching the churches established at Antioch, Bangor, Ireland; Iona, Scotland; Hernnhut, Saxony (Germany). What marked them all was their commitment to worship and prayer, many of them day and night. It is reported that the Bangor Monastery had almost 200 years of non-stop worship and prayer and Hernnhut had over 100 years. They were committed to teaching the word of God and operating in signs and wonders. They trained, equipped and sent out believers. These "Apostolic Centers" became beachheads for influence of the Kingdom of God in a region and from there the world was changed. That is our model.

We need "Apostolic Centers" that will raise up believers who are on fire for Jesus. Those who have paid the price in intimacy with Him through spending committed time in worship and prayer. However, these believers must also be solidly grounded in the word of God, trained up to move in signs and wonders then be released full of faith to go and transform every sphere of society.

It's Your Turn:

Pray that the Lord would raise up these "Apostolic Centers" and leaders to be great equippers of the Saints for the works of the ministry, both inside and outside the walls of the church building.

If you are a Pastor or Leader of a Ministry consider setting aside a season for non-stop worship and prayer. It will change the life of the people in your church or ministry.

Consider researching and studying some of the historic "Apostolic Centers" I mentioned.

Read Ephesians 4:7-13.

Day 6

Arizona's Economic Revival
Cindy Jacobs- July 2005

"And the Lord says to Arizona I am taking you to a place of economic revival. When other states go down, I'm going to bring you up. The Lord says the silver is mine and the gold is mine, and I'm getting ready to release treasures of darkness from the earth. I'm getting ready to release wealth even into my Body. There are those who for decades have fought to try to transfer wealth. There are those who for decades have had an anointing with the gift of giving, even a Joseph anointing, but it seems as if there was not a breakthrough but God says I, the great Breaker, am coming. And I am coming to tread down the enemies of poverty and lack."

It is interesting that at the time this word was released; Arizona was in a time of great prosperity. The housing market was on an upswing and life was good. However, often times a word gets released and all of a sudden things seem to go in the opposite direction. After this word was released Arizona suffered greatly as a result of the economic crash of 2008.

This can happen with us as individuals too. Sometimes we receive an amazing prophetic promise and things in the natural seem to be diametrically opposed to what was released in the prophetic word. We can even see this played out in the lives of many in Scripture. Since Joseph was mentioned in this word, we should look at his life. Joseph went from having prophetic dreams of leadership to being thrown in a pit and sold as a slave!

It is an encouragement to us that in 1 Timothy 1:18 Paul admonishes Timothy to wage war with those prophetic words. Just like the State of Arizona, you may have received a prophetic word concerning your personal finances but your bank account is not reflecting that word, lay hold of that promise and start waging war.

I have to give a little side note concerning prophesy over your personal finances. Please make sure you are following the Biblical principle of tithes and offerings. The Lord will not override His precepts if we aren't being obedient in this area.

As for Arizona, we are primed to see the Lord move mightily where only He can get the glory for our economic recovery.

It's Your Turn:

Ask the Lord to come with His breaker anointing to see the breakthrough in Arizona's economy.

"The one who breaks open will come up before them;
They will break out, Pass through the gate, And go out by it;
Their king will pass before them, With the LORD at their
head." Micah 2:13

Read Malachi 3:6-12 and ask the Lord if there is any place where you are robbing Him.

Day 7

Favor Eruption
Graham Cooke- June 2010

"The church in Arizona will have never seen favor like this in its existence, EVER. There is a favor erupting over this state which if my people will take hold and pull it down it will change the dimension of this state spiritually forever. It will change the government of this state, it will change the way business will be done in this state. It will bring reformation into your culture, into your society. If you will pull down from heaven all that heaven has suspended, you will see this state radically altered."

In Strong's Exhaustive Concordance favor, in the New Testament is the Greek word "charis". One of the definitions of "charis" is divine influence. Thayer's Greek-English Lexicon goes on to expound the same word to denote extraordinary powers. According to Baker's Evangelical Dictionary of Biblical Theology one of the meanings of favor is special benefits or blessings. Psalm 68:19 states, *"Blessed be the Lord, Who daily loads us with benefits."*

We need all the extraordinary power, divine influence and benefits we can lay our hands on if we hope to see reformation of the culture in our state. What an amazing

25

promise this prophetic or "rhema" word holds. Add to that the power of the "logos" or written word that the Lord DAILY loads us up with benefits! Wow!

There is an eruption of favor suspended over us. If we would just reach up and lay hold of it and pull it down, it would change our state forever. Let's reach up and pull down this eruption of favor into Arizona's Government, that they would seek the wisdom of the Lord and His benefits to govern this state with righteousness and justice.

Then there is business and commerce. If we are going to see Economic Revival, we need supernatural ideas and strategies just like Joseph had that ultimately saved his nation.

Finally, there is the Church! We need a favor eruption in the way we function. As individuals and as the corporate church we need to walk in the favor of the Lord and all His benefits. Oh, that we would be endued with His power to impact those around us and bring heaven to earth and see our state radically changed. Favor will look differently for each one of us depending upon the sphere of influence the Lord has given us.

It's Your Turn:

Lord, I declare that I am reaching up to pull down that eruption of favor over my life, my family, my church, my workplace or school and the government of Arizona.

Lord, I thank you that DAILY you load me up with benefits. Give me eyes to see those benefits and bless you for them.

Make a list of the benefits you receive from the Lord today!

Day 8

Get the Airports and Transit Systems Ready!
Chuck Pierce – November 2009

"Get the airport and transit system ready for the next move of God to begin. The worlds eyes are on you (AZ) and they even saw your stadiums one way. They will be on you again in the next 5 years and your stadiums will be seen worldwide for the move of the spirit that I AM bringing. So rise up and usher Me in."

During the first planning meeting for "The Torch" non-stop prayer initiative, we knew that the Lord's heart was to have non-stop prayer, not only inside the church but also outside. Since that meeting in 2007 we have helped mobilize non-stop prayer in every sphere of society including schools, hospitals, businesses and jails. We have even rented hotel rooms and prayed in casinos.

We waited patiently for the release from the Lord to mobilize non-stop prayer at Sky Harbor International Airport. For two years we prayed. Then this word was released and we knew it was a confirmation for non-stop prayer at the airport. But, the Lord continued to tell us to wait.

29

Early in 2013 we felt we finally had the "yes" from the Lord. The reality was that we could have gone and prayed and nobody would have been any the wiser, but that was not the leading we were sensing from the Lord. We felt we were to ask for permission from the governing authorities. The Lord blessed us with great favor and He opened an amazing door for us to mobilize a week of non-stop prayer at the airport.

We built an altar of worship to the Lord in a location that stands on original Hohokam land. The Hohokam are the original indigenous people of the Phoenix metropolitan area. We know from history that the Hohokam were avid sun worshippers, but we were there to worship the SON, Jesus! We pressed into the prophetic word to prepare the airport for the coming move of God.

As we mobilized and prayed for 168 hours one of the key scriptures we declared was Psalm 24:7. At this ancient Hohokam gate that is now one of the main entry points into our state, we declared the ancient gates to open up so that the King of Glory could come in!

It's Your Turn:

Lord, we ask that you send many to continue to pray onsite at our airports to prepare the way for You.

Lift up your heads, you gates; be lifted up, you ancient doors, that the King of glory may come in. Psalm 24:7 (NIV)

The voice of one crying in the wilderness: "Prepare the way of the Lord; Make straight in the desert a highway for our God." Isaiah 40:3

I want to encourage you anytime you are at the airport or ride a bus to pray and prepare the way for the move of God in Arizona.

Day 9

Opening the Gates
Randy DeMain – 2007

"Out of this region is going to be the opening authority for the Northwest and the Southwest gates spiritually. Phoenix is the gate that is going to release a great move. This place has the authority to open the Northwest and the Southwest gates to usher in the move of God, usher in revival, usher in a great outpouring the likes of which have not been seen in the earth."

I enjoy looking up the meaning of words. I know looking up the meaning of the word "gate" may seem a bit elementary. But, I thought what I found was interesting. By definition it is a structure that can be swung, drawn, or lowered to block an entrance or a passageway. An opening in a wall or fence for entrance or exit. The structure surrounding an opening, such as the monumental or fortified entrance to a palace or walled city. It is a means of access.

Researching gates in scripture is also a fascinating study. Business was conducted at the gates. Gates represented a place of authority. Public announcements were made and court was convened there. Biblically, gates have great symbolic importance. The only way to lawfully enter a city was through its gates. To control the gates of your enemy meant that you had control of the city. When a conquering king entered the city by the gates, it meant he had gained control and authority of all its assets and resources.

While researching for the Sky Harbor International airport prayer assignment, I discovered quite an amazing visual image. From an aerial perspective, at the eastern gate of the airport, you can see the image of a coiled rattle snack almost like a tattoo on the land. I'm sure the designers of the landscaping surrounding the airport thought it might be a nice touch to incorporate some artwork from the original indigenous people. However, I believe it is very symbolic of how the serpent would like to sit at one of the gates of our state and try to control it. I know you may think I'm stretching things a bit, but hopefully you will give me the luxury of this interpretation. The fun thing is that from that same aerial view you can also see that an overpass looks like it symbolically cuts off its head. That's what we do when we pray!

It's Your Turn:

Declare Genesis 22:17, *"With blessings I will bless you, and multiplying I will multiply your descendants as the stars of the heaven and as the sand which is on the seashore,* **and your descendants shall possess the gate of their enemies.** *"*

Declare that the Northwest and Southwest gates of this Continent will be open to usher in the move of God.

Ask the Lord to show you the gates you are to possess.

Day 10

Glory Cloud
Charles Shamp – August 2012

"The Lord spoke to me and said, "America will see My cloud touch down in the desert in this season." As I sat on the plane I saw in a vision the hand of God in a cloud come down on the desert; it stretched from Reno all the way to Phoenix. It released a light that could be seen all over and people that lived as far as the East Coast were talking about the light of God that was in the desert. I watched as people from all over America went out to the desert region to be baptized into His cloud of glory."

When this word was first released through a prophetic website, it brought me great encouragement. At the time, I was struggling through an intense season of personal warfare. I was thankful for this word and was determined all the more to press in to see the glory cloud of the Lord, not only for me but for the state.

So many of the prophetic words that have been released over Arizona have been about the "glory". Here is just a sampling, many of which haven't made it specifically into this book, but look at the promises of the glory: "Being a prototype for glory", "being the only state fully engulfed and on fire with the glory", "Arizona to become the greatest glory dwelling place in the USA", "Arizona is the key glory carrier for the 50 states." Wow!

As I think about the "glory" I can't help but have the song by Jesus Culture "Show me Your Glory" flood my soul. "I see the cloud and I step in, I want to see your glory as Moses did." I am reminded of being a brand new Christian and the first scripture I ever prayed was Exodus 33:18, "And he said, "Please show me your glory". "I guess I was a "glory junky" before I knew what a glory junky was! Nineteen years later my heart's cry is still "Lord, show me your glory!" Is that the cry of your heart too?

It's Your Turn:

Are you willing to pay the price of intimacy with the Lord to see His glory? Are you willing to embrace the fire to be carriers of His glory? There is always a cost. I want to encourage you to meditate on these scriptures on the "glory". Then listen to the Jesus Culture song "Show me Your Glory". If you can, listen to it multiple times until it truly becomes your heart's cry.

Read and meditate on the following Scriptures: Exodus 33:18-33, 2 Chronicles 7:1-3, Psalm 72:19, Isaiah 6:1-4, Habakkuk 2:14.

Day 11

Children's Revival
Cindy Jacobs – July 2005

"I am going to begin a move even among in the elementary schools. I'm going to raise up children's intercessory prayer groups. And in the first graders, second graders, third graders I am coming with angelic visitations. You mark it down... there will be a day in the Arizona Republic the headlines will say "Children Seeing Angels...Can Angels go to School?" Because God says I am the Famous One and I will be glorified in all the earth."

I asked a dear friend of mine, Linda L'Amoreaux to write today's section. Linda has served the children of Arizona as a teacher, a pastor and a mother. I wanted to honor her along with all those who serve Arizona's children.

It all started with a simple chess competition. I was the teacher in charge of the chess club for my campus. The kids loved it! The challenge was engaging, but the biggest draw was simply being with their friends and having genuine conversation. I often listened as they shared with each other and laughed. It was refreshing! On a Friday near Spring Break, I overheard a budding conversation about Easter. "What is Easter? I know about the bunny and the jelly beans, but what is it really all about?" Her opponent was caught off guard and responded, "Are you serious? You don't know what Easter is?" And then he didn't miss a beat! I heard him tell her that Easter was the celebration of Jesus rising from the dead. He told her all about the crucifixion and how God must really love us. He explained what sin is and how, "We all got it". She kept asking and he kept answering. By the time chess club was over, he had led her to Christ in my classroom. I knew I was watching prophesy being fulfilled. My school had just been shaken for the Glory of God!

Today, I am a children's pastor. In Children's Church we have experienced the presence of angels, smelled the sweet aroma and felt the air move around us. Children hear His voice and pray with authority. They are giving words from the altar and interpreting them with adult-like clarity. They are praying against illness with fervency. A new move of God is being birthed in our kids. They are a new Samuel generation who will prophesy and restore the Word of the Lord to their generation; in Arizona and to the nations!

It's Your Turn:

I want to encourage you to see your children in a new light today. Children are primed to know Jesus and recognize His presence. Let children teach you how to play. Join them on the Kingdom playground. Spend time at the family altar. Learn to worship with wild abandon. Learn how to see and live the simple message of love. He is moving in our kids and His Spirit is being poured upon them.

"Then after I have poured out my rains again, I will pour out my Spirit upon all people. Your sons and daughters will prophesy. Your old men will dream dreams. Your young men will see visions." Joel 2:28

Day 12

Prototype for Glory
Chuck Pierce - September 2012

*"The State of Arizona is going to be first prototype of glory. New winds of the spirit coming through the desert, there will be many haboobs. They will be uncovered and they will come. They will get drinks and be re-clothed in the oasis with new spiritual life on them. Worship in a new way and see healings at the oasis. Arizona **WILL** be a glory state; the desert will blossom."*

"Haboob" is an Arabic word meaning blasting. It is a type of intense dust storm. A haboob is a wall of dust that is the result of a microburst or downburst. The air that is forced downward is pushed forward by the front of a thunderstorm cell. The sights of these haboobs are almost surreal and can be quite disturbing if you are caught in the middle of one.

The force and power of this wind and storm reminds me of how Psalm 29 describes the voice of the Lord. It says that the voice of the Lord is so powerful that it can strip the forest bare, causes deer to give birth and the wilderness to shake, all while His people cry glory!

Sometimes when those haboobs hit our lives and it seems like everything is being shaken. We must remember that in the midst of the shaking there will also be a birthing of the promises we are carrying if we remember to give God the glory.

There is so much to unpack in this prophetic word but I really want to focus on how we worship when the winds come. The beginning of Psalm 29 says to give the LORD the glory due to His name and to worship the LORD in the beauty of His holiness. The prophetic word says to worship in a new way and see healings at the oasis.

It's Your Turn:

I want to encourage you to worship in a new way today.

Maybe your worship will be a time of quiet and solitude, even on a hike along one of the many beautiful trails we have in the wilderness of Arizona (or your own place of beauty wherever you may live) and meditate on Psalm 29.

Maybe it will be singing at the top of your lungs in total abandonment making the declaration as David did in 2 Samuel 6:21 "And I will be even more undignified than this".

Or maybe it will be meditating on the Word of God and worshipping the Lord in the beauty of His holiness.

Whichever new way you choose to worship the Lord today, my prayer for you is for you to see His glory in a new way. We as individuals have to become prototypes of His glory before the state can see the fulfillment of this word.

Read and meditate on Psalm 29, 1 Chronicles 16:29, Psalm 96:9.

Day 13

Isaiah 35

Isaiah 35:1, 5-6
Wilderness and desert will sing joyously; the badlands will celebrate and flower—Like the crocus in spring, bursting into blossom, a symphony of song and color... Blind eyes will be opened, deaf ears unstopped, lame men and women will leap like deer, the voiceless break into song. Springs of water will burst out in the wilderness, streams flow in the desert. Hot sands will become a cool oasis, thirsty ground a splashing fountain. [The Message]

I have been in countless gatherings over the years where one prophetic voice after another has prophesied Isaiah 35 over the State of Arizona. During my research I have seen it noted that the landscape of Arizona is very similar to that of Israel, so I find it interesting that this Scripture would be prophesied so often. This passage of scripture has some amazing promises of the Lord; deserts blooming, blind eyes seeing, lame walking just to mention a few. To me it is a picture of the fullness of the revival that the Lord longs to bring to our state.

When I moved to Arizona from England and I had a preconceived idea of what the desert would look like. I expected sand dunes and something looking like the Sahara Desert of North Africa. I was quite shocked to see just how much life there is in the "deserts" of Arizona. I was even more shocked to see the desert explode in color after the winter rains. I picked "The Message" version of the Bible for this quote for today because I enjoyed the expressiveness of the language it used.

During the "Start the Year Off Right" gathering hosted by Hal and Cheryl Sacks of Bridge Builders International in 2013, the worship team released a prophetic song about the Desert Rains. I have included the lyrics below. Arizona let's arise and see our deserts bloom.

Desert Rain
Though darkness invades and the enemy pursues,
No weapon that's fashioned will overtake you,
Cause the glory is falling anew upon you in desert rain.
Arise, shine; break off the fetters that are holding you down.
Come alive, fly, ascend and take your place in the glory realm.
For rivers will flow in the dry land and I'll flood its banks by the power of my hand.
The desert rejoices and blooms again as I go before you, with desert rain
He goes before you so rise and shine, he goes before you, lift up your eyes
Arise, shine; break off the fetters that are holding you down.
Come alive, fly, ascend and take your place in the glory realm.

It's Your Turn:

Meditate and pray through Isaiah 35. Consider reading it in several different versions of the Bible.

Listen to the song "Desert Rain" on YouTube
http://www.youtube.com/watch?
v=WIfnPsaccEo&feature=youtu.be

Day 14

Re-digging the Wells
Maria Woodworth-Etter - 1913

"We are not yet up to the fullness of the Former Rain and that when the Latter Rain comes, it will far exceed anything we have seen!"

I'm taking some literary license on this word as it is not Arizona specific; however I believe we should all be praying for this. I included this word in the collection for a lot of personal reasons but to also share about the great history of healings, miracles, signs and wonders we have in this State. It is part of our heritage; there are deep wells here in Arizona.

My husband, Jack, is Maria Woodworth-Etters great (x3) grandson. For those of you who may not have heard of her, she was a nineteenth-century healing revivalist. She walked in amazing signs, wonders and miracles and saw thousands upon thousands saved as she preached the message of divine healing. It is reported that she carried such an anointing of the Lord that the presence and power of God sovereignly touched people up to 50 miles away from her meetings.

After Jack moved here from Indiana, we found out that Maria had actually been in Arizona and held 8 weeks of revival meetings that rocked Phoenix in 1908. We researched and found an article in the Assembly of God Archives attributing the establishment of the Pentecostal movement in Arizona to Mother Etter.

After Mother Etter, came other such heroes of faith as Franklin Hall, William Branham and A.A. Allen. I know that some of these may not have finished well in our eyes; however we cannot dispute that the Lord used them mightily in our State. The legacy of signs and wonders is our inheritance.

"And Isaac dug again the wells of water which they had dug in the days of Abraham his father, for the Philistines had stopped them up after the death of Abraham. He called them by the names which his father had called them." Genesis 26:18

Are we willing to re-dig the wells of healing and miracles that are in the land? Just like Isaac, we may face some contention and resistance but are we willing to keep pressing in like he did until we too can declare, "For now the LORD has made room for us, and we shall be fruitful in the land."

I believe that each of these heroes were forerunners of the greater promise to see an army of Marias, Halls, Branhams, etc. be raised up for such a time as this!

It's Your Turn:

Declare that the healing wells in Arizona be reopened, in Jesus Name!

Read and meditate on Psalm 105:1-11, Hosea 6:3 , Zachariah 10:1, and Joel 2:23.

Study some of these heroes of the faith and the impact they had in Arizona.

Day 15

City of Refuge
Clara Grace -1965

In a vision, Sister Grace was in California and the earth begun to shake and move and the coastal area started falling into the ocean. She started to run, she ran past Glendale and Palm Springs and got by Indio but could run no further. At the time of the vision, she was 85. The Lord instructed her to keep running. When she finally stopped running she turned around and looked up. The clouds of destruction and despair where so heavy. She then turned to the eastern states and she saw clouds of invasion. She looked to the northwest and saw the same thing. Clara asked the Lord if He would allow the entire Nation to be overcome. Then she saw legions of angels joining the ranks of the believers and together they overcame the invading forces. It left America victorious but deeply wounded. The Lord then instructed Clara to take this vision to three cities and prophesy this vision. The three cities were Phoenix, Dallas and Tulsa. That was the order. She was to prophesy these cities would be cities of refuge and strongholds of evangelism for nations of the world.

This retelling of the vision was given recently at a prayer meeting by world renowned prayer walker, Henry Gruver. Brother Henry was present in that Phoenix meeting in 1965 when Sister Grace originally shared the vision. He recounted that it was as fresh in his mind that day as it was when he first heard it 49 years earlier. The 1965 vision was a continuation of a vision that Sister Grace had in 1948.

I know of many prophetic voices that over the years have also prophesied that Phoenix would be a city of refuge. Long before I knew any of these "city of refuge" words existed, I had a very intense encounter with the Lord where I saw in a vision droves of people pouring into Arizona. Interestingly enough in the vision I saw them coming from the west. It reminded me of the scenes on the television when the news stations reported on Hurricane Katrina. We were inundated with pictures of thousands of people migrating to safety.

I am not trying to presume that California is going to fall into the Ocean. However, because of the numerous accounts of similar visions and prophesies we have to ask the Lord for wisdom. But more importantly, from my own encounter I realized that it would take much preparation for Phoenix and Arizona to be ready to fulfill this prophesy. Even now my hearts cry is for the Lord to prepare us in the natural and in the spiritual so that we don't miss our assignment.

It's Your Turn:

Pray for the Lord to release wisdom within the Church and government on how to be prepared and positioned to be a city of refuge.

Consider taking a seminar on disaster preparedness. This is a practical step to prepare you and your family for any kind of emergency.

Day 16

The Righteous Cry
Eve Nunez - 1974

"In the last days saith The Lord, I will visit your City of Phoenix. A Baptism of fire will baptize both young and old, it will start like a spark and spread like wildfire throughout The State of Arizona. The eyes of The Lord are upon the Righteous, in this City of Phoenix and My ears are open to their cries. It will be known as a "Godly City" all over the World. I will pour my Glory upon the inhabitants of this City and surrounding cities and purify you with my Fire. It will be called the City of the Son, not the city of the sun. The Righteous cry, and The Lord hearth, and I will deliver them out of all their troubles. The Lord is near to them that have a broken heart; and a contrite spirit. Many are the afflictions of the righteous; in this "City of Phoenix" says The Lord but I will deliver him out of all of them. You will be a City of Refuge, you must welcome the stranger, care for your orphans and the widows."

Eve is a dear friend of mine and it was an honor to have her included in this publication. I felt it was important to have representation from the Hispanic community. I could have written on several different aspects of this word, but felt impressed to connect with Eve's heritage and to pray for one of Arizona's most challenging problems. As I spoke with Eve about her word, I was so touched by her heart for the downtrodden and also of her stories of how she has prayed and served Arizona since she was a young girl. She also shared about the history of Phoenix and a special Hispanic woman. So, in a few short paragraphs I will attempt to thread these thoughts together.

Jack Swilling, the founder of modern day Phoenix's second marriage was with a young Mexican woman of Spanish heritage named Trinidad Mejia Escalante. They had seven biological children, five girls and two boys, and like the prophetic word states they adopted and cared for two orphaned Apache children. Eve shared that she recalled her dad speaking often about the founders of Phoenix as she was growing up. In December 1925, The Arizona Republican reported the death of Trinidad Escalante Swilling. She was 78 years old. The article stated that she was one of the best-known pioneer figures of the Salt River Valley. People speak often of Jack, but forget his better half Trinidad. As Eve recalls, "We Hispanics call Trinidad the "mother of Phoenix"."

Phoenix and Arizona are a melting pot of diverse cultures. It has nations both within and outside its borders. Prior to the Gadsden Purchase of 1854, Phoenix would have been considered a border town as the Gila River marked the separation of the United States and Mexico. Arizona continues to be embroiled in a complicated battle concerning immigration issues and the safety of our border. However, in the midst of this we cannot forget that there are the innocent and the oppressed caught in the crossfire. We should not forget our mandate to be a city of refuge to care for those in need. I will be the first to admit there is no easy answer. However, I believe the Lord has a solution. We must appeal to heaven for the Lord's heart on this matter and continue to pray for His justice, not mans.

It's Your Turn:

Read and meditate on Isaiah 58, Jeremiah 22:3 and Jeremiah 29:7.

Pray for wisdom for those in authority to navigate this difficult issue.

Day 17

A Prophetic Word for the Navajo Nation
Kay Winters - 2012

"For the Lord would say to the Navajo Nation: "I am coming in this hour to you as your Healer. Indeed, I will close and stitch up the gaping wound of betrayal. Although as a nation you have been cast aside and left for dead in an ash head of grief and hopelessness. I shall heal your bruised soul and broken spirit. Surely I have seen your affliction and heard your cry. As you reach for the hem of My garment, I will heal your wounds of injustice, and fill your land with My glory."

For the Lord says, "The wounds of devastation shall no longer haunt you, for I have paid the price of your healing. Indeed, the "Long Walk" of yesterday shall no longer be to you a shadow and shroud of shame, for you shall walk upon the high place of honor and glory."

As I continued to pray through this writing project, I knew I had to search out a prophetic promise for the Native People of Arizona. We have to have completeness and we have to honor the original people of the land. Although this word was specifically released to the Navajo Nation, I believe it is the Lord's heart to see healing come to all the First Nations in Arizona.

To give you a little background; Arizona has twenty one federally recognized tribes. According to the 2000 Census, Arizona is home to over 250,000 Native Americans and the reservation and tribal communities comprise over a quarter of Arizona's land mass.

During a meeting in 2013, it was released that there are still strongholds in the state that are linked with broken covenants and the first people. We still have much work to be done with repentance, reconciliation and restitution within the borders of Arizona and our First Nations People.

In Chuck Pierce's book "Reordering Your Day: Understanding and Embracing the Four Prayer Watches," he especially suggests praying through the Third Watch if there is a covenant breaking spirit in the region that you live. The Third Watch is known as the "Breaking of a Day" or "Cockcrowing Watch" and is from midnight to 3:00 a.m. He goes on to suggest doing the watch for 21 days as it was the number of days it took Daniel to breakthrough in prayer. (Reference Daniel 10:12-14)

It's Your Turn:

Chuck said in the same book that he didn't have a specific prayer focus for the Third Watch. I would like to suggest that you take this book and use it as a resource. Let's pray during the Third Watch and let strategy break forth to see the covenant breaking spirit's stronghold removed from Arizona!

Pray for strategies of repentance, reconciliation and restitution for the First Nations of Arizona.

Consider spending some time with the Lord and meditate on the covenant we have with Him and take Communion.

Day 18

Model of Genuine Unity
Brian Alton - 2005

"For Arizona has yielded herself to my testing, and now, has received my blessing. In this state, there are key men and women who have been completely apprehended by my Spirit, and I will sovereignly bring them together for a greater purpose and destiny than their own. I am releasing a Corporate Anointing, an anointing that resides upon all of them together. A passionate praising, praying, faithful people who are in one mind, and in one accord, unified in spirit and in my Kingdom purpose and plan for this state. For the Lord would say that the anointing that rests upon you Arizona is far greater 'together' than any anointing that rests upon any one person, church, or group. You will become a model of true and genuine unity - a message of unity to this whole nation."

It comes as little surprise to me that the enemy has worked so hard to bring disunity to the body of Christ. He knows that if we could come together as Jesus prayed in His "High Priestly" prayer in John 17 we would be a force to be reckoned with. In Genesis 11:6 it states, *"And the LORD said, "Indeed the people are one and they all have one language, and this is what they begin to do; now nothing that they propose to do will be withheld from them."* The context of this Scripture is obviously from a negative standpoint. The people had evil in their heart; however, there is a principle here about unity. They had one language, in the Hebrew it also means to have the same words. Matthew 18:19 says, *"Again I tell you, if two of you on earth agree (harmonize together, make a symphony together) about whatever [anything and everything] they may ask, it will come to pass and be done for them by My Father in heaven..."* [Amplified Bible] There is great power in unity!

In every revival I have studied; unity has always played an integral part. However, you can't have unity without two other key components: humility and love. To see this new model of genuine unity arise we need a new baptism of love. Love for Jesus and love for one another. As 1 Corinthians 13:4-7 says, *"Love suffers long and is kind; love does not envy; love does not parade itself, is not puffed up; does not behave rudely, does not seek its own, is not provoked, thinks no evil; does not rejoice in iniquity, but rejoices in the truth; bears all things, believes all things, hopes all things, endures all things."* We cannot unify around a cause or a project; that will only prove to be temporary. We must have a unity birthed out of love and humility. Then the world will see that we are Christians by our love.

So how does love, humility and unity get birthed? Honestly I don't have the answer, but what I do know is when we come together to praise and worship the King of Kings with no agenda but to bring glory to Him, who is worthy, the Lord will visit. The more time we spend together in His presence, the more we become like Him. It's a good place to start.

It's Your Turn:

Lord, we cry out for a fresh baptism of your love.

Read and meditate on Psalm 133 and John 17.

Consider gathering with other believers, not necessarily from your own fellowship to worship.

Day 19

The Golden Net
Henry Gruver - 1979

"In a vision I was looking at the City of Phoenix. I could see Ahwatukee, Buckeye, Apache Junction and the White Tank Mountains. I could see massive angels at each corner of the City, and I could see a golden net. The angels were holding each corner and it was draped over the entire valley. I went into intercession and was crying out for the angels to drop it because I knew it meant harvest. The Lord said, "I will not give orders to drop the net until Pastors of this area come together with a common vision for this Valley and the souls here"."

Henry Gruver is an amazing man of God and in my opinion he is one of God's stealth weapons! Brother Henry is known as the father of the prayer walking movement. He has prayer walked the globe and prayed in some amazing places. I love hearing stories of his exploits.

Henry has strong connections to my home church, but I whimsically liken him to "Where's Waldo". He truly could be anywhere in the world at any point in time, but I am amazed by God at how He orders the steps of the righteous. As I prayed, researched and inquired during the process of compiling the prophetic words for this book I knew Henry had a key. I have quite a history of Henry showing up at church just when I need him. So, I reminded the Lord of how He had done that before and waited with excitement to see how the Lord would work. I was not disappointed! Within three days of starting to pray who showed up at Wednesday morning prayer? You guessed it, Brother Henry! Thirty Five years later I was able to hear the vision straight from Henry. I share part of the story with you to encourage you in your faith that the Lord hears our prayers.

So, back to the vision. Henry shared that he believes the net is still suspended over the valley. It is yet another prophetic word that is hovering over us just like the golden net. It was encouraging to know that it was still there, but we must be diligent to pray for the Pastors and Leaders in the valley to unite with the common vision to harvest the souls.

It's Your Turn:

Pray for your Pastor to be one of those who would have a heart to come together with other Pastors and seek the Lord's heart for a vision for the souls in this valley or where ever you may live.

If you are a Pastor, Leader or someone who has influence, consider gathering others to seek the Lord. I believe this is not to be limited just to those in the church, but also those with influence in other spheres of society.

Pray for the Lord to release the net at that opportune moment in time to reap the greatest harvest.

Read and meditate on John 21:6-11 and Ezekiel 47:7-10.

Day 20

Canopy of Praise
Pete Ngai – August, 2006

"There is a fire coming out of Flagstaff and a fire coming out of Tucson and there will also be a move of God coming from eastern Arizona and from western Arizona. I am lifting up a pillar of praise in Phoenix and I am putting tent pegs in Flagstaff, Tucson, western Arizona, and eastern Arizona and I am forming a canopy of praise, a covering over the state that will break the curse over the land."

This word was given during an intense season of contending for righteous government for the State of Arizona. There was a remnant team which was fasting and praying non-stop for 40 days. There was much revelation that came out of that season concerning Arizona and strongholds that needed to be dealt with as well as some redemptive promises such as this prophetic word.

As I have travelled throughout the State of Arizona mobilizing prayer, I have heard multiple people give an account of a very similar vision. I have heard it described as looking like a patchwork quilt as different expressions of praise and worship to our Lord.

Over the years I have been blessed to be a part of many different worship and prayer services and to see the beautiful diversity of the Bride of Christ. It could be the simplest of services with acapella worship and a handful of people or a full praise team and thousands; in all flavors and expressions of Christianity from conservative mainline denominations to charismatic; and everything in between. All I can say is how beautiful His Bride is and the canopy of praise that is being woven together.

I also believe that as this canopy of praise is erected it will also provide a protective covering over Arizona. For years, I have seen the numbers "911". I'm sure many of you reading this see certain numbers in a similar way. We know that "911" is an emergency number and it is also the date that memorializes a tragic event. After seeing this number over and over, I finally asked the Lord why I kept seeing these same numbers and what was He telling me. He had me look up two passages of scripture.

"On that day I will raise up the tabernacle of David, which has fallen down, and repair its damages; I will raise up its ruins, and rebuild it as in the days of old." Amos 9:11

"He who dwells in the secret place of the Most High shall abide under the shadow of the Almighty." Psalm 91:1

These verses seem appropriate to apply and pray for Arizona.

It's Your Turn:

As well as praying through this prophetic word and the "911" scriptures consider attending a worship service at a congregation that is outside your usual affiliation and be blessed as you see worship expressed in a way that you are less familiar with.

Day 21

Arizona Now Is Your Time!
Rebecca Greenwood – January, 2014

"Arizona, now is your time. There is a wind of the Spirit that is blowing across your state releasing a new wave of unity. Where there has been a disrupting of relationships in the past season, in this season there will be a move and forming of covenantal relationships that will lead the way for a new move of God. He is giving you keys of authority to see that structures that have set themselves against covenantal kingdom relationship in the state overturned. There is a hunger for His holiness and fire that knit hearts together in a supernatural way. A new wave of healing is breaking forth, a healing river and fire anointing that will stir hearts of men to run to the Lord's presence and goodness. A fire of the Lord's presence is resting over Arizona and will ignite a passion in the hearts of men that cannot be quenched. The torch of the Lord has sealed this state as one who will lead the nation in experiencing in His glory, presence and holiness. Arizona now is the time!"

We still continue to contend with a covenant breaking spirit in this land, but I am bold enough to say that I believe we are making headway. I believe as we continue to worship and pray we will continue to gain strategies to see these strongholds brought down.

At the end of a season of night watches in 2011, the Lord gave me a picture of a rusty lock with a big key in it. I then saw the oil dripping off Aaron's beard flowing into the lock. Psalm 133:1-2 *"Behold, how good and how pleasant it is For brethren to dwell together in unity! It is like the precious oil upon the head, running down on the beard, the beard of Aaron."*

The Lord explained that as we worship together in unity it will unlock the things that have been held up over this region. I know this is a key to seeing the glory manifest. No wonder the enemy has tried so hard to devastate covenant relationships, especially those among believers!

I felt as I finished this book we needed to end with a fresh word from the Lord. While I was developing the original outline, I had the word from Becca Greenwood slotted for Day 21. Becca has ministered multiple times in Arizona and loves this state, so I asked her to pray and write a prophetic word especially for this project. How fitting that her prophesy would start with "Arizona now is your time!"

It's Your Turn:

Father, I thank you that you are forming new covenant relationships and giving us keys of authority to see those structures in this state that have set themselves against covenant relationships overturned. I thank you that you are going to release a healing river and fire anointing on this state that will stir hearts to run into your presence. I thank you that you have sealed Arizona and that we will lead the nation in experiencing your glory, presence and holiness.

Thank you Lord that NOW IS OUR TIME!

APPENDIX

"The Torch" Non-Stop Prayer Initiative

The vision of The Torch is to unite God's people by establishing non-stop prayer coverage in a region and see revival and transformation come. God is calling His people to intimacy and unity through The Torch non-stop prayer initiative!

The original vision was to organize and equip 52 local teams in Arizona who would each cover one week of non-stop prayer in 2008. Similar to the passing of the baton in a relay race, the "prayer torch" is passed to a new prayer team each week. For each week, the team commits to cover all-day, all-night prayer from some pre-determined location. Our desire was to see non-stop prayer happen in churches, hospitals, universities, daycares, airports, businesses, jails and that has happened.

Leviticus 6:13—"The fire shall be burning continually upon the altar; it shall not go out."

We longed to see *Arizona* transformed as *Arizonans* are transformed and see God's Kingdom expand on the earth. We long to see the Torch not only blaze throughout Arizona but throughout the United States and into other nations. In unity, the walls come down when we pray together across denominational, cultural and generational lines and in all spheres of society.

Your prayer week should be broken into comfortable time slots depending on your prayer group. This could be ½ to 2 hour slots allowing people to sign up for multiple slots. Prayer time can include personal or corporate worship time, silent personal prayer, group prayer, worshipful music playing; anything that glories God and ushers in His Presence. *Seek the Lord and ask Him for a plan for your week! One of the keys is to provide a creative environment that promotes prayer and worship.*

The youth are a great untapped resource for prayer. They are hungry for something bigger than them and are underwhelmed by the church. They are an inspired generation that will go for it if they can catch the vision.

We have chosen to focus on seeing God's people united in prayer for revival and transformation in Arizona; however, we also desire to give freedom to the Holy Spirit to direct prayer to whatever is on the heart of God at the moment. Revival breaks out among us when the focus of our prayer time becomes simply to enter into the presence of God and to be transformed by that intimate relationship with Him.

"IT STARTED WITH ONE HOUR!"—

"This truly is the new wineskin for 24-7 Prayer."
Che Ahn, HIM/Harvest Rock Church

"Arizona, the Lord has seen your sacrifice and He is sending His blazing Torch... Don't let this go out.. it will be a model for the Nation."
Dutch Sheets, Dutch Sheets Ministries

"The vision for the "Torch" was remarkable when it started, but half way through that first year it seemed to accelerate. It

took off. We must recognize that at the heart of this vision is Jesus Christ."

Pete Greig, Author of Red Moon Rising

"*In 25 years of ministry, the week of on-stop prayer is one of the most significant things I have personally participated in.*"

Pastor Guthrie Boyd

"*In worship on Thursday night there was a significant, let me repeat significant outpouring of the Spirit of God!*"

Chaplain Steve Martinez - Pima County Jail

"*We are experiencing the 'rain' from the awesome prayer week. The whole environment was 'different'. We had a baptism at the lake. There were 6 signed up; 20 people got baptized. One man was wearing nice clothes. He came walking into the water and was baptized. Is there a difference after the 24-7 prayer week...YES!*"

Robert B. Candelaria – Page, AZ

If you are interested in hosting a week of non-stop prayer or want to receive training to be equipped for a season of non-stop prayer we can help! Contact our ministry office at pray24-7@litethefire.org.

CREDITS:

Some prophetic words have been slightly modified for the purpose of developing this devotional, however great care has been taken to not change the intent or integrity of the original word. Credits for prophetic words given to:

Brian Alton – Desert Rose Christian Fellowship, Gateway International Bible Institute
www.drcconline.org / www.gibionline.org

Randy DeMain – Kingdom Revelation Ministries
www.kingdomrevelation.org

James Goll – Encounters Network
www.encountersnetwork.com

Clara Grace

Rebecca Greenwood- Christian Harvest international, SPAN
www.christianharvestinlt.org

Henry Gruver

Cindy Jacobs – Generals International
www.generals.org

Rick Joyner – Morning Star Ministries
www.morningstarministries.org

Peter Ngai – Hand of Mercy Apostolic Center
www.handofmercy.org

Eve Nunez – Help4Kidz and Arizona Latino Commission
www.help4kidz.org / www.arizonalatinocommission.com

Chuck Pierce – Global Spheres/Glory of Zion
www.gloryofzion.org

Hal & Cheryl Sacks – Bridge Builders International
www.bridgebuilders.net

Charles Shamp – Destiny Encounters
www.destinyencounters.com

Kay Winters – Prepare the Way International
www.preparethewayint.com

Maria Woodworth-Etter
www.facebook.com/m.b.woodworth.etter

ABOUT DEB WELCH

 Deb Welch – Founder / Director – Lite the Fire

Deb is passionate about mobilizing and equipping the body of Christ to engage in an intimate, fiery relationship with Jesus. The Lord called her to be a "fire-starter" and in 2006, she launched Lite the Fire. Deb and her husband Jack lead the ministry together. They facilitate "The Torch" non-stop prayer initiative and are also the Arizona State leaders for SPAN (Strategic Prayer Action Network), a global prayer network lead by Becca Greenwood, Christian Harvest International.

Deb has written articles for Pray Magazine and Breaking Christian News, developed numerous training materials, speaks at conferences and schools and has led prayer teams to pray onsite both within the US and Internationally.

The Vision of Lite the Fire is to Ignite the Generations for Breakthrough and Transformation through prayer, impartation, training and activation.

To invite Deb to minister contact Lite the Fire at:

pray24-7@litethefire.org

13954 W. Waddell #103, PMB 179
Surprise, AZ 85379
www.litethefire.org

Made in the USA
Middletown, DE
13 August 2020

15232551R00057